Belair Early Years Design & Technology

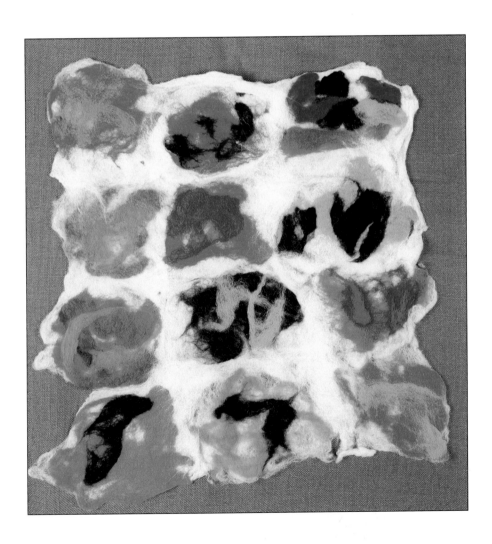

Hilary Ansell

Acknowledgements

I am indebted to Anna McAdams and Helen Spowage, teachers at Kingfisher Primary School, for all their help and encouragement and without whom this book would probably not have been written. Many, many thanks to you both. Thank you also to all the children in their respective classes who have been such a delight to work with. I think much fun was had by all!

Thank you too to my friends at St John's Hospice for your constant support and encouragement.

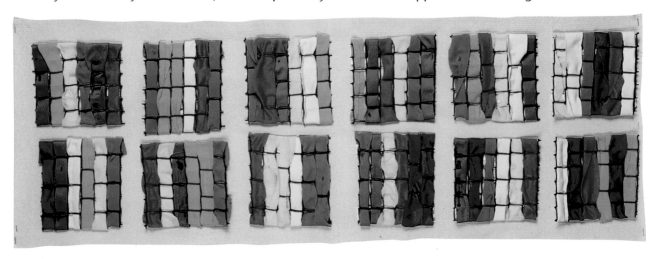

Make it with Mesh (page 36)

Published by Collins, An imprint of HarperCollins*Publishers*
77 – 85 Fulham Palace Road, Hammersmith, London, W6 8JB

Browse the complete Collins catalogue at
www.collinseducation.com

© HarperCollins*Publishers* Limited 2012
Previously published in 2007 by Folens
First published in 2003 by Belair Publications

10 9 8 7 6 5 4 3 2 1

ISBN-13 978-0-00-744797-8

Hilary Ansell asserts her moral rights to be identified as the author of this work

British Library Cataloguing in Publication Data
A Catalogue record for this publication is available from the British Library

All Early learning goals, Areas of learning and development, and Aspects of learning quoted in this book are taken from the *Statutory Framework for the Early Years Foundation Stage*, Department for Education, 2012 (available at www.education.gov.uk/publications). This information is licensed under the terms of the Open Government Licence (www.nationalarchives.gov.uk/doc/open-government-licence).

Every effort has been made to trace copyright holders and to obtain their permission for the use of copyright material. The authors and publishers will gladly receive any information enabling them to rectify any error or omission in subsequent editions.

Cover concept: Mount Deluxe   Cover design: Linda Miles, Lodestone Publishing
Cover photography: Nigel Meager   Commissioning editor: Zöe Nichols
Editor: Helen Oakes   Design: Jane Conway
Page layout: Philippa Jarvis   Photography: Roger Brown and Marcus Pomfret

Printed and bound by Printing Express Limited, Hong Kong

MIX
Paper from responsible sources
FSC
www.fsc.org   FSC™ C007454

Contents

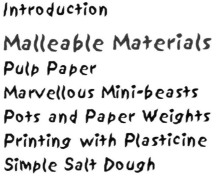
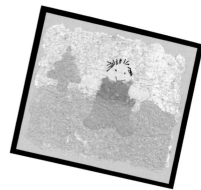

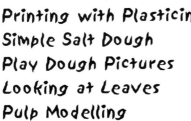

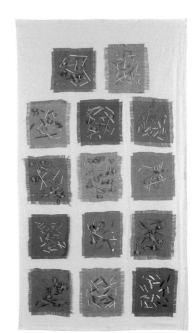

3

Introduction

The **Belair Early Years** series has been well-loved by early years educators working with the under-fives for many years. This re-launched edition of these practical resource books offers popular, tried and tested ideas, all written by professionals working in early years education. The inspirational ideas will support educators in delivering the three characteristics of effective teaching and learning identified in the Statutory Framework for the Early Years Foundation Stage 2012: playing and exploring, active learning, and creating and thinking critically.

The guiding principles at the heart of the EYFS Framework 2012 emphasise the importance of the unique child, the impact of positive relationships and enabling environments on children's learning and development, and that children develop and learn in different ways and at different rates. The 'hands on' activities in **Belair Early Years** fit this ethos perfectly and are ideal for developing the EYFS prime areas of learning (Communication and language, Physical development, Personal, social and emotional development) and specific areas of learning (Literacy, Mathematics, Understanding the world, Expressive arts and design) which should be implemented through a mix of child-initiated and adult-led activities. Purposeful play is vital for children's development, whether leading their own play or participating in play guided by adults.

Throughout this book full-colour photography is used to offer inspiration for presenting and developing children's individual work with creative display ideas for each theme. Display is highly beneficial as a stimulus for further exploration, as well as providing a visual communication of ideas and a creative record of children's learning journeys. In addition to descriptions of the activities, each theme in this book provides clear Learning Intentions and extension ideas and activities as Home Links to involve parents/carers in their child's learning.

This title, **Design and Technology**, supports children's progress towards attaining the Early Learning Goals in a number of areas of learning, Expressive arts and design (exploring and using media and materials), Communication and language (listening, understanding and following instructions), Physical development (control and co-ordination and the handling of equipment and tools effectively), Personal, social and emotional development (self confidence and self awareness) and Understanding the world (the use of technology in the home and in schools).

Children whatever their age love making things. They need time to explore and experiment with a wide range of materials and they derive great satisfaction from an end result. The ideas presented in this book provide an opportunity for the children to develop and extend a range of techniques such as cutting (using scissors or pastry cutters), tearing, joining (using paste, PVA glue, tape, staples and by sewing), modelling

(with clay, salt dough, play dough, paper pulp) and experimenting with a range of textile techniques such as weaving and rug prodding. As the children develop these skills, so too will they gain in confidence.

While the children are working on projects their vocabulary can be extended through discussion. There are many opportunities for the use of comparative and evaluative language development.

Some skills will need to be taught and the children always need to be reminded about safety issues when using tools such as scissors, needles and hammers.

I hope that adults and children alike will enjoy exploring the activities in this book.

Hilary Ansell

Pulp Paper

Learning Intentions

- To see how materials can change.

- To use simple tools.

- To learn about recycling.

Starting Points

- Ask the children to look around the room and identify the ways in which paper has been used. Can they think of other uses? For example, wallpaper, tablecloths, paper towels, serviettes, toilet paper and kitchen rolls.

- Examine a variety of different types of paper. Do any of the children know how paper is made? Briefly explain. Tell the children how old papers can be shredded and used again to make new paper.

- Shred and tear old coloured tissue and display paper, ready to be made into new paper.

Designing and Making

- The paper pulp is made by liquidising torn scraps of paper. The children will be able to help with the tearing but it is better to have some of the colours prepared beforehand.

- Have prepared some simple paper making frames. These are made easily by stapling sheets of aluminium mesh to wooden frames. Simply cut four lengths of wood to size and glue and staple together. Balance the frames across shallow trays to catch the water.

- Set out containers of coloured pulp and spoons. Ask the children to create patterns on the mesh simply by spooning different colours of pulp onto the frames.

- Small turkey basters are also fun to use and create spots and splatters of colour.

- When the mesh is covered and the excess water has drained through, simply tip the frame upside down onto a kitchen cloth on a wad of newspaper (the newspaper is to soak up the water). Gently lift off the frame and pat the sheet of pulp with a sponge thus drawing up the excess water.

- Place another kitchen cloth over the sheet of pulp and more newspaper. Repeat the process.

- At the end of the day, separate the kitchen cloths containing the pulp from the newspaper and leave to dry overnight in a warm place. Gently peel the sheets of paper off the cloths; they can be ironed flat while still damp.

Development

- Use pastry cutters to incorporate shapes into the designs. Simply place the cutter on the mesh and spoon the desired colour into it. Fill up the rest of the frame as before.

- Make a paper shape mobile. Place shaped cutters on the mesh and fill with pulp. Press down to squeeze out as much water as possible. Carefully remove the cutters and turn the shapes onto kitchen cloths and dry as described above. When dry thread the shapes together and hang to create a mobile.

Home Links

Ask parents or carers to:

● allow children to cut out pictures from catalogues and magazines of things made from paper

● encourage children to look for products while out shopping that are made from recycled materials.

Display

● Mount the brightly coloured papers onto black and display in clip frames.

● Mount and make into calendars or cards.

● Mount the paper shapes on contrasting paper and use as greetings card fronts.

● Hang the mobile where it will catch a current of air and move gently.

Marvellous Mini-beasts

Learning Intentions

- To discover the properties of clay.

- To discover that materials can change and that these changes are irreversible.

- To develop fine motor skills.

- To learn about mini-beasts and their habitats.

Starting Points

- Walk around the school's grounds to look for mini-beasts. Can the children suggest the creatures that they might find and where they might find them?

- Bring snails and worms into the classroom in a specimen box with a magnifying lid and explain that this will enable them to see the creatures more clearly. House them safely in a fish tank with a fine mesh lid. (Always return mini-beasts to the wild after the session.)

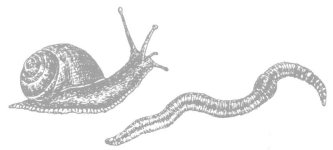

Designing and Making

- Provide soft clay and allow plenty of time for the children to experiment with it. Encourage them to knead, squeeze, mould and roll.

- Create worms, snails and other mini-beasts using the clay. Show the children how to join pieces of clay with slip. Relate this to other gluing experiences.

- Encourage comparisons. This worm is longer than that worm. This slug is fatter than that slug.

- Make coil pots by coiling their 'snakes' around a circular or oval base of clay. Demonstrate how to smooth the coils together.

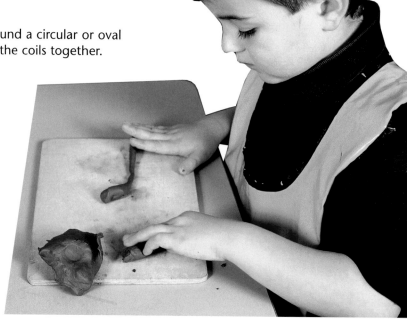

Development

- Provide an assortment of craft materials such as pipe cleaners, short lengths of florist's wire, scraps of coloured acetate, stiff net and tissue. Ask the children to think about making creatures with legs and wings. How will they join these to the clay?

- Develop the idea of rolling worms of clay into snakes. Make long wavy snakes and coiled snakes.

- Make a real wormery in the classroom so that the children can study the worms at work.

Display

- Create a 'pretend' wormery by putting a layer of soil or potting compost into a glass tank. Place a few leaves on the surface. Poke some clay 'worms' into the soil and lay others on the surface. Arrange the other 'mini-beasts' on the leaves.

Home Links

Ask parents or carers to:

- help the children to identify mini-beasts at home or in the park

- provide opportunities for the children to play with play dough or modelling clay at home.

Pots and Paper Weights

Learning Intentions

● To introduce shaping, joining and decorating techniques.

● To learn to use tools to help shape and decorate the clay.

● To design and make small decorative articles.

Starting Points

● Ask the children to look for examples of pottery around the home: cups, saucers, dishes, bowls, plates, vases and ornaments. If possible have some examples of handmade pottery to show them. Look at the ways in which they are decorated.

Designing and Making

● Roll a lump of clay in the hands until it makes a round ball.

● Press the thumb into the centre of the ball and squeeze the sides gently until the ball has opened up to become a pot. Be careful not to squeeze the walls of the pot too thin.

● Ask the children to choose tools with which to make marks in the clay (pencil point, end of a paint brush, a paste spreader, and so on).

● Create texture by adding small pellets of clay and thin coils using slip to join.

● Demonstrate how clay can be pressed through a strainer or garlic press to create shreds of clay, which can be used to decorate the pot.

● Paint with ready-mixed paint when completely dry.

Development

- Make a pinch pot but do not decorate. Turn it upside down on the table and decorate by poking with a pencil. Paint when dry and use as a paperweight.

- Use self-hardening clay to make a pottery pendant. Roll the clay flat with a rolling pin. Cut out a simple shape and decorate by poking with a pencil. Pierce a hole at the top of the pendant. Paint when dry. Varnish. Thread with a coloured lace.

Display

- Create a display area of various levels using boxes. Drape with a plain fabric that sets off the colours of the pots. Arrange the pots putting dried flowers in some and short pencils in others to demonstrate the usefulness of the children's creations.

- Paint a small branch and set in plaster. Hang the pendants on this.

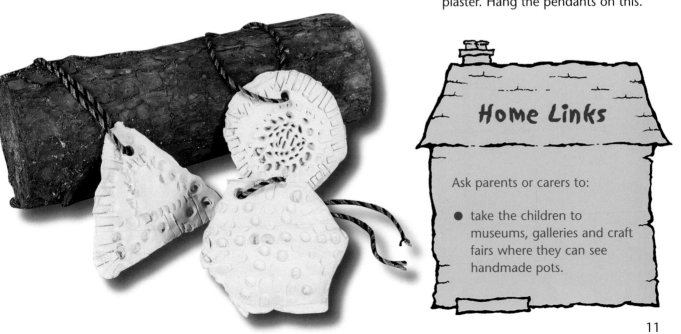

Home Links

Ask parents or carers to:

- take the children to museums, galleries and craft fairs where they can see handmade pots.

Printing with Plasticine

Learning Intentions

- To make their own tool with which to print.

- To develop fine motor skills.

- To develop an awareness of colour.

Starting Points

- If possible, examine a selection of manufactured printing blocks and decorators' stamps, including blocks from a variety of ethnic backgrounds.

- The children will already have experience of printing with bottle tops and other everyday objects. Can the children find things about the classroom or home that have a printed pattern on them?

Designing and Making

Making the block

- Have available an assortment of shallow lids.

- Roll the plasticine into 'worms' and small balls.

- Make arrangements of these in a lid. Encourage the children to experiment with arrangements until they are satisfied.

- When the lid is completely filled, press down on the plasticine with a smooth hard surface, to ensure that the balls and worms are level. The shapes should merge slightly but not disappear.

Printing

- Use squares of bright and pastel coloured paper and pots of poster or ready-mixed paint.

- Use a soft brush to apply a thin layer of paint to the printing block. Do not apply too much paint. Place the square of paper on top of the block and press down firmly. Carefully peel off the print. Try taking a second impression without adding further paint. This is often more successful than the first.

Development

● Discuss other materials that could be used for printing. Provide rectangles and circles of thick card to use as a base for the printing block. Have available a wide range of materials such as thick string, scraps of sponge, screwed up paper, bits of fabric, lentils, rice, lace and ribbon. Discuss the suitability of various types of glue, while sticking the scraps to the base. Encourage the children to use scissors to modify the scraps provided.

● Try printing with scrunched up pieces of bubble wrap, newsprint or fabric. Using natural colours creates a texture similar to that of walls and stones.

Display

● Use finished prints as wallpaper for the role-play corner.

● Look at examples of modern art. Mount arrangements of the prints in clip frames and hang on the wall.

● Use the bubble wrap prints to create stones to be used in displays of natural objects. Simply cut a stone shape from the print. Staple another piece of paper behind this and stuff the shape with scrunched up paper or plastic bags.

Home Links

Ask parents or carers to:

● bring lids from jars and containers into school

● help the children to identify printed patterns about the home on furnishing fabric, wallpaper and clothing.

Simple Salt Dough

Learning Intentions

- To discover that materials can change and that the change is irreversible.

- To experience mixing techniques.

- To learn to knead, roll and shape.

Starting Points

- Look at each other's faces. Ask the children to close their eyes and feel with their hands over their own face and decide which bits stick out and which bits go in.

- Name each feature and help them to establish whereabouts on the face the various features are located.

Designing and Making

- Working in a small group, ask a child to measure out 1 cup of salt and 3 cups of plain flour. Talk about the difference in texture between the flour and the salt. Add 1 cup of cold water and take turns in mixing until the dough has formed. Divide the lump of dough and ask the children to knead and roll the dough on a floured board until it is smooth. Talk about how the dough feels.

- Take a handful of dough, roll and flatten it to make a face shape. Poke holes into the dough where the eyes should be. Create a mouth, nose and ears and stick them into position using a little water.

- Can the children suggest how to make hair from dough? Roll very thin 'worms' of dough and fix in place for strands of hair or squeeze dough through a garlic press.

- Bake the dough on the lowest setting of the oven until it is absolutely dry.

- Paint when cold. Varnish or paint with PVA to prevent the dough absorbing moisture from the atmosphere.

14

Development

- Turn the dough faces into fridge magnets by gluing small magnets to the back.

- What kind of a house does their dough character live in? Make house plaques. Roll the dough to a thickness of about 1cm. Cut out a house shape. Roll thin sausages of dough and use these to outline the window shapes and the door.

- Draw different faces on circular paper.

- Discuss what else could be used to make faces. Make collaged faces with buttons, beads, wool and raffia.

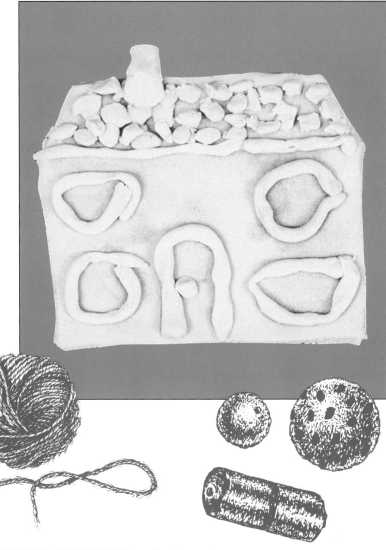

Display

- Use double-sided tape to display the dough faces and houses alongside the children's 2D drawings.

Home Links

Ask parents or carers to:

- provide an opportunity for the children to model with salt dough at home.

Play Dough Pictures

Learning Intentions

- To practise rolling and cutting techniques.

- To recognise shapes, i.e. circle, square, triangle, rectangle.

- To combine shapes to make simple pictures.

Starting Points

- Ask the children to find examples of shapes around the room – for example, doors, windows, wheels on cars.

- Examine a selection of objects and talk about how they are made up of more than one shape.

- Experiment with tesselation using small plastic shapes to make pictures.

Designing and Making

- Make up quantities of coloured play dough allowing the children to help with the measuring and stirring.

- Have ready a variety of shape pastry cutters, bottle tops and plastic pots of different sizes. Ask the children to roll out small quantities of dough and cut out a variety of shapes.

- Give the children a sheet of brightly coloured card on which to build their picture and let them experiment with combinations of shapes.

- Experiment with cutting some shapes in half. What other shapes can be made?

Development

● Introduce a story element into the picture-making. Provide shape cutters such as trees, animals and people. Ask the children to make a house for a dough character using the shapes available. Add trees next to the house and other cut-outs, such as animals.

● Make edible pictures by cutting shapes out of biscuit dough. The children could pretend to be giants eating the village! Encourage them to create stories.

Display

● The play dough pictures are temporary creations but could be displayed for a short while. Display on a table top with a background of shape posters. Create levels using boxes or large play bricks. Intersperse the pictures with several shape cutters.

Home Links

Ask parents or carers to:

● help the children identify circles, triangles, squares and rectangles at home or in the community

● provide opportunities for the children to help make biscuits or pastry at home

● encourage the children to look for and cut out shapes from catalogues or magazines.

Looking at Leaves

Learning Intentions

- To extend clay techniques to include rolling and cutting.

- To use simple tools.

- To learn that leaves can be different shapes.

Starting Points

- Ask the children to describe what a leaf looks like. Do they appreciate that leaves can be different shapes and that each type of tree or plant has its own particular leaf shape?

- Take the children for a walk around the school grounds to look for different leaf shapes.

- Discuss how leaves change with the seasons and how some trees lose them altogether. The children will make a permanent record of some leaf shapes by pressing them into clay.

Designing and Making

- Have ready leaves of different shapes and sizes with well-defined vein patterns on the underside. Encourage comparison of size and shape, introducing words such as longer, rounder, fatter, thinner and more pointed. Discuss texture with words such as glossy, smooth, velvety and crinkly.

- Roll out the clay to a thickness of about 1cm. Press the veined side of the leaf firmly into the damp clay. It can be rolled over with a rolling pin. Help the children to cut around the leaf shape. Gently remove the leaf. The clay leaf can then be left flat or the edges can be lifted slightly to give a more natural appearance. Paint or glaze when dry or fired.

Development

- Pierce holes at the stem end of the clay leaves before drying. Thread the leaves and create a mobile.

- Make a decorated tile or wall plaque by first rolling out and cutting a square of clay. Then press and cut out a leaf shape from slightly thinner clay. Attach this to the tile with slip. Remember to pierce a hole at the top of the tile for hanging.

- Make a teapot or pan stand by pressing a leaf into a square or circle of clay. Remember this must be fired and glazed if it is going to be used. Glue a piece of felt to the bottom to prevent scratching.

- Make a pendant or brooch. Choose a small leaf. Roll a ball of soft clay in the palms of the hands. Put the leaf face down on the clay board. Put the ball of clay on top of it and squash the clay flat. A small block of wood could be used to press the clay to ensure that the back is flat. Remember to make a hole for the lace. If making a brooch, glue on a fastening pin after firing or when it is completely dry.

Display

- Thread the leaves with coloured yarn and hang as a mobile or window decoration.

- Make wax leaf rubbings and display with the clay and real leaves.

- Create greetings cards by gluing a small clay leaf onto a scrap of hessian and sticking this to the front of the card.

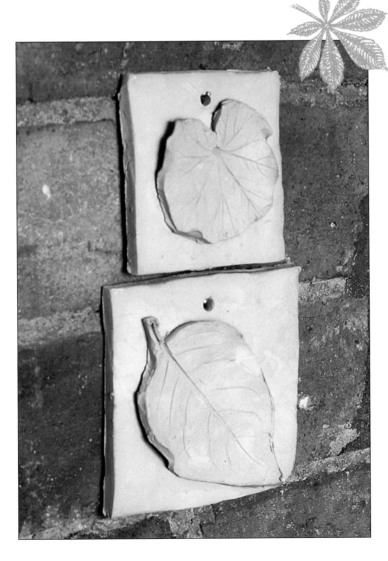

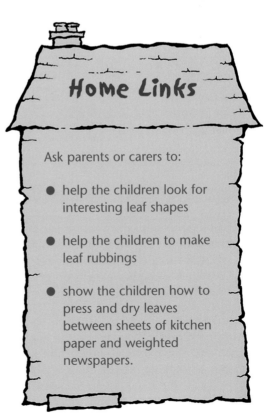

Home Links

Ask parents or carers to:

- help the children look for interesting leaf shapes

- help the children to make leaf rubbings

- show the children how to press and dry leaves between sheets of kitchen paper and weighted newspapers.

Pulp Modelling

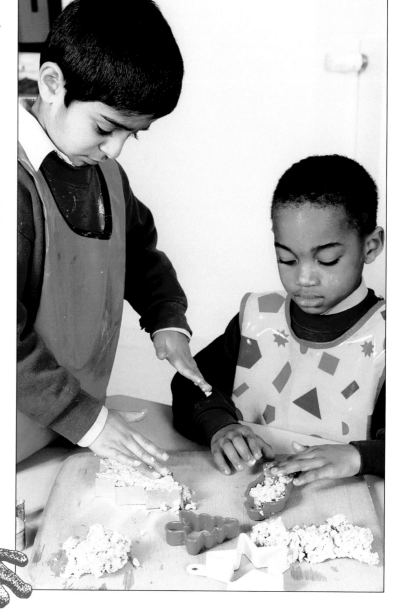

Learning Intentions

● To discover that paper can be used as a malleable modelling material.

● To use simple tools.

● To discover that some materials change when they become wet.

Starting Points

● Ask the children if they have ever been out in very heavy rain. Talk about what happened to their clothes. Some may say the water soaked through their clothes.

● Do clothes feel different when wet? Explain that some clothes 'absorb' water. Experiment with other materials that absorb water. Provide the children with different types of paper, plus some water to play with.

Designing and Making

● Use scrap paper or soft white paper to make the pulp. Ask the children to tear the paper into small pieces. Add sufficient hand hot water to cover the paper. Let the children squeeze and knead the paper. Press with potato mashers until the paper disintegrates. Squeeze off excess water through a colander or sieve and add a little cellulose adhesive. Keep the mixture firm.

● Have ready a range of pastry cutters of different shapes (including stars) and let the children press the pulp into the cutters filling them to the top. Make sure that the pulp is pressed down well. Gently push the pulp shape out of the cutter onto a tray or plate. The shapes can then be left to air dry or put into the microwave on medium for short intervals – 5, 3, 1 minute(s) – with 5-minute intervals between for the steam to evaporate. Take great care if using the microwave not to scorch the paper. Do not leave unattended.

Development

● Choose a theme and cut templates from card, for example animals, butterflies, transport or reptiles. Press paper pulp onto the card shape until it is full. Paint when dry.

● Take the theme of a jungle or farm and make paper pulp animals on card templates. Then paint or sponge a suitable background and glue on the animals.

● Make clay models. Roll out the clay and use the shape cutters to create people and animals. Gently smooth down the fine edges on the front of the shape to give a more rounded appearance.

Display

● Arrange the shapes on simple coloured backgrounds to create pictures and glue down.

● Spray or paint the star shapes silver and mount on deep blue paper.

Home Links

Ask parents or carers to:

● help the children make paper pulp and model with it at home. This can be done without the addition of cellulose adhesive

● encourage the children to identify absorbent materials.

Crafty Curtains

Learning Intentions

- To identify circular shapes.

- To develop spatial awareness.

- To learn how circular shapes can be repeated and combined to make an image.

Starting Points

- Ask the children to identify circles and circular shapes in the classroom. Have they seen other circular shapes elsewhere?

- Make a collection of circular shaped objects suitable for printing such as cotton bobbins, small lids, bottle tops or corks.

Designing and Making

- Provide a selection of circular printing objects and ready-mixed paint in primary colours. Lay out sufficient white or pale cotton fabric to make the curtains. (If the curtains are likely to be washed at a future date, fabric medium can be mixed with the paint to fix it.)

- Dip a shape into the paint, make sure it is not dripping and press firmly onto the cotton fabric. Lift off carefully.

- Repeat using different colours and different sized shapes until the fabric is evenly covered. Encourage the children to look for the spaces and gauge whether their shape will fit.

- Discuss shapes. Did some shapes print better than others? Why?

Development

- Introduce the use of straight lines (e.g. short lengths of wooden beading, thick and thin card) with the circles. Practise printing on paper. Ask the children if they can make pictures using straight lines and circles.

- Make flower pictures by printing smaller circles all the way around larger ones. Finish with stick prints for the stem and leaves.

- Make arrangements of concentric circles and turn into flowers. Ask the children to start with the largest circle they can print and work down in size finishing with a dot (print with a pencil end).

Display

- Gather the length of printed fabric and use as curtains for the home corner.

- Make a skirt for a table and display the collection of circular objects.

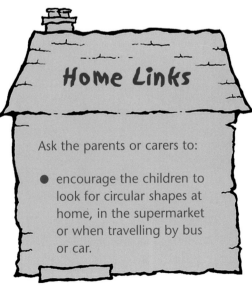

Home Links

Ask the parents or carers to:

- encourage the children to look for circular shapes at home, in the supermarket or when travelling by bus or car.

Tufty Textures

Learning Intentions

- To become familiar with the feel of different types of fabric.

- To increase manual dexterity.

- To identify names of colours.

Starting Points

- Examine the clothing that the children are wearing. Do all fabrics feel the same? Is a particular fabric smooth, soft, rough, warm, cool?

- Identify other fabrics in the room. Which is their favourite texture?

- Introduce the names of various fabrics such as satin, velvet, cotton and wool. Do they know that wool comes from a sheep and cotton comes from a plant?

- Talk about shades of a colour. Are all blues the same? Discuss light blues and dark blues. How many different blues (or any other colour) are there in the classroom?

Designing and Making

- Have available 10cm square pieces of rigid plastic garden mesh and short strips of a variety of fabrics sorted according to colour. The strips need to be 10cm in length but the width can vary according to the thickness of the fabric.

- Show the children how to poke one end of the strip through a hole in the mesh and then poke the other end through the hole next to it. Pull both ends level. Repeat this until all the holes are filled.

- Explain that people used to make rugs in this way but they used fabrics rather than plastic mesh. Show the children samples of rug canvas and hessian. Compare the size of the holes in the three materials.

Development

- Create texture panels in the same way using other materials, such as strips of plastic bag, rug wools, string, lace, florist's ribbon or even sweet wrappers and foils.

- Try poking holes in hessian with a pencil or the end of a paint brush and pushing strips of fabric through them.

Display

- Mount squares on contrasting coloured paper.

- Assemble plastic squares to make one large wall hanging sorting according to colour. Try horizontal, vertical or diagonal arrangements.

- Using fabric glue, stick rug canvas squares onto a hemmed hessian background and use as a rug in the home corner.

- Create pictures out of the finished squares by trimming and gluing to card backgrounds.

Home Links

Ask parents or carers to:

- examine textiles around the home with their children looking for different textures such as towelling, fur fabric, cotton and woollens

- identify the uses of textiles: curtains, duvets, towels, face cloths, rugs, carpets, clothes and toys.

Creating on Canvas

Learning Intentions

- To develop hand/eye co-ordination.

- To learn to use a simple tool.

- To learn the basics of stitching.

- To judge which colours stand out against others.

Starting Points

- Ask the children if they have seen anyone sew with a needle and thread. Perhaps they have seen members of the family sew on buttons.

- Discuss how clothes are sewn together from separate pieces of fabric.

- Talk about and show examples of embroidery and stitching.

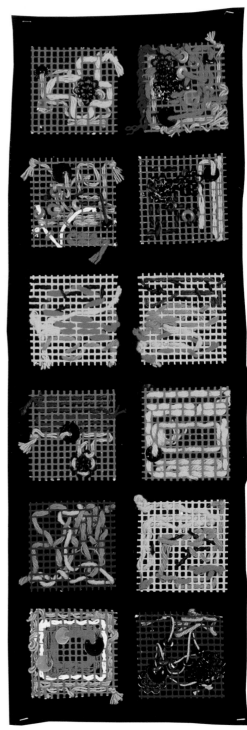

Designing and Making

- Paint squares of rug canvas in primary colours. Leave to dry.

- Provide fat large-eyed needles.

- Using coloured laces, thick embroidery cotton or wool, start by tying the thread to the edge of the canvas. Ask the children to stitch down one hole and up through another anywhere on the canvas. In this way, make stitches of different size and direction. It often helps to keep repeating "Down from the front and up from the back."

- Encourage the children to choose colours that stand out against the colour of the canvas. Introduce the term 'contrasting colours'.

⚠ **Note:** Supervise the use of needles.

Development

- Attach objects with holes such as large beads, shells, washers, curtain rings or sea-worn pebbles.

- Stitch in lines up and down the rows of holes. Create patterns by missing different numbers of holes, e.g. up through one hole, miss two and down through the next.

- Repeat the main activity using coloured hessian instead of rug canvas.

Display

- Join the patches of sewing to make the fronts of cushions for the home corner. Decorate with ribbon.

- Join patches with beads to create an interestingly-textured wall hanging.

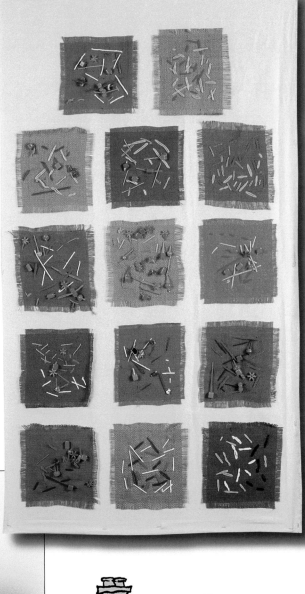

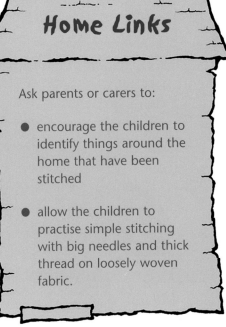

Home Links

Ask parents or carers to:

- encourage the children to identify things around the home that have been stitched

- allow the children to practise simple stitching with big needles and thick thread on loosely woven fabric.

Soft Sculptures

Learning Intentions

- To explore the possibilities of 3D textile work.

- To introduce simple toy making techniques.

- To explore textures.

- To develop an awareness of pattern.

Starting Points

- Examine several simple soft toys and discuss how they are transformed from flat to 3D shapes.

- Explain to the children that they are going to make their own stuffed toys using old tights and socks. Encourage discussion about how they can do this.

- Look at pictures of exotic snakes and caterpillars.

- Discuss with the children what they might use to stuff the toys. Ask them to bring to school thick coloured tights and socks of all sizes.

Designing and Making

- Help the children to cut the legs off the tights.

- Have available a choice of stuffing materials such as scraps of fabric, polyester toy filler, scraps of sponge/foam, scrunched up newspaper and plastic bags. Ask the children to feel each of the prospective fillers and decide which would be the most suitable for their particular creature. Introduce words such as hard, soft, lumpy and scratchy.

- When the snake is stuffed, help the children to tie off or sew up the open end.

- Have available a range of craft materials such as scraps of felt or pre-cut circles and triangles, sequins, buttons, small craft pompoms, feathers and pipe cleaners. Ask the children to decorate their creatures. Draw their attention to the repeated patterns on the snakes in the pictures.

Development

- Before decorating, tie the basic snake shape into segments to create a caterpillar. Then decorate.

- Create fantasy creatures with wings, fins and horns.

- Ask the children to give their creature a name. Discuss with the class what it eats, where it lives and what it does.

- Encourage the children to tell stories about their creatures.

Display

- Hang the creatures in a jungle corner in the role-play area.

- Cover a table top with sand-coloured paper or fabric. Sprinkle with sand and pebbles. Add a few rocks and some leaves. Place some twigs towards the back of the table top. Twist some snakes around the twigs, prop the caterpillars against the leaves and place the other snakes amongst the rocks.

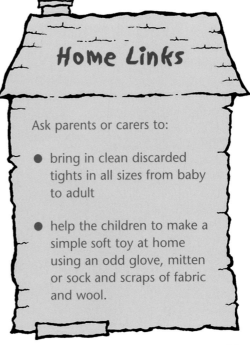

Home Links

Ask parents or carers to:

- bring in clean discarded tights in all sizes from baby to adult

- help the children to make a simple soft toy at home using an odd glove, mitten or sock and scraps of fabric and wool.

Peg Loom Patchwork

Sets of plastic peg looms are available from school suppliers. Handcrafted sets in wood are sometimes found in craft shops.

Learning Intentions

- To introduce the concept of weaving.

- To use simple apparatus to help achieve an end product.

- To understand how some fabrics are made.

- To develop fine motor skills.

Starting Points

- Ask the children to examine their clothes. Are all the fabrics the same? Do they know what knitting is? Maybe someone has seen a member of the family knitting and can describe this to the class.

- Explain that fabric can be made in many ways. Talk about weaving and show the children a loom, wool and a finished piece of weaving.

Designing and Making

- Prepare the peg looms according to the manufacturer's instructions.

- Have available a variety of thick wools such as chunky knitting wool and rug wool. Young children can obtain a rapid result using thick wools.

- Demonstrate how to wind the wool in and out of the sticks. Weave until the piece is about 10cm deep.

- Pull the sticks up through the weaving so that the weaving slides down onto the warp threads. Tie the warp threads in pairs at each end of the weaving and trim off the ends.

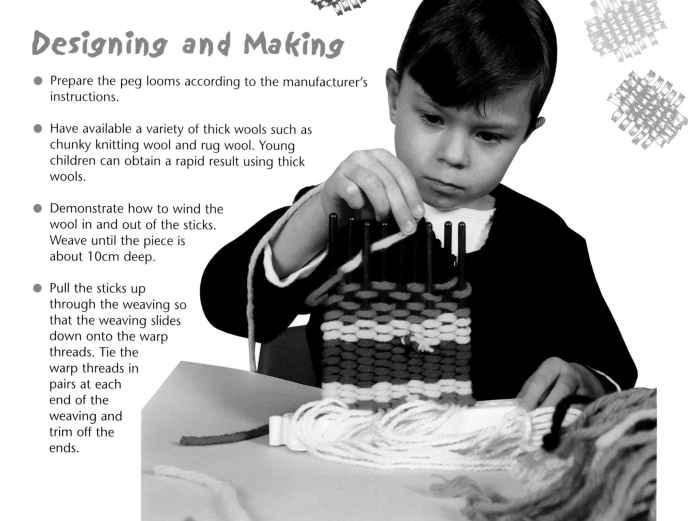

Development

- Thread the loom with longer warp threads and weave to create a long decorative panel instead of small pieces.

- Try weaving with strips of soft fabric or plastic bags. Let the children suggest different materials that they could use.

- Introduce weaving on a 'flat loom'. Cut strips of thin coloured card. Create a loom by gluing or stapling the ends of these to a contrasting sheet of card to form the warp strips. Show the children how to weave over and under the warp strips and slide the weft strips down to the bottom.

Display

- Use the individual weavings to create cards and calendars.

- Sew or glue the small squares onto a hemmed backing fabric and use as a cover in the home play area, or alternatively use as a cushion front.

- Join the small pieces together and use as a wall hanging. Hang side by side with the longer panels.

- Weavings incorporating fabric and plastics could be glued onto hessian using latex glue and used as a small mat in the home corner.

Home Links

Ask parents or carers to:

- bring into school oddments of thick wool, ribbon, lace, coloured plastic bags and soft fabrics to use in the weavings

- help the children to identify woven fabrics around the home.

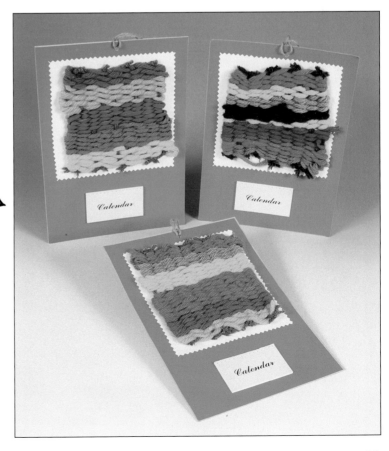

First Felt

Starting Points

● Explain that some fabrics come from plants, some come from animals and others are manufactured. Have examples of cotton, silk, wool and acrylic to show the children.

● Show them a picture of a sheep. Ask if anyone has actually seen a live sheep or even touched one. Talk about its thick fleece and have a sample of natural fleece to show the children. Explain that woollen fibres are called tops.

Designing and Making

● Pass around a handful of coloured tops and feel how soft it is. Demonstrate how the fibres cling together with water. Ask the children to tease out the fibres and lightly roll them into a ball in the palms of their hands.

● Lightly sprinkle the tops with water that has a drop of washing up liquid added to it. Roll the ball of tops around and around in the hands until it shrinks and tightens and becomes quite firm. Did the children expect this to happen? Rinse well.

● To make a piece of felt, tease out the tops and lay a thin layer of fibres horizontally on a piece of bubble wrap. On top of these lay another layer of fibres in a vertical direction. Place a third layer of fibres in a horizontal direction. Cover with a piece of curtain net. Sprinkle with soapy water and rub with a circular motion until the fibres start to knit together.

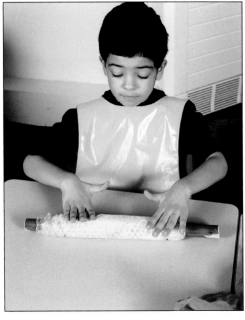

● Carefully pull off the net and roll the wet felt and bubble wrap around a length of broom handle. Secure the ends with elastic bands and roll backwards and forwards on the table. The more you roll, the more the felt will shrink and thicken. When you are satisfied that the fibres are holding together, rinse well in clear water and leave to dry.

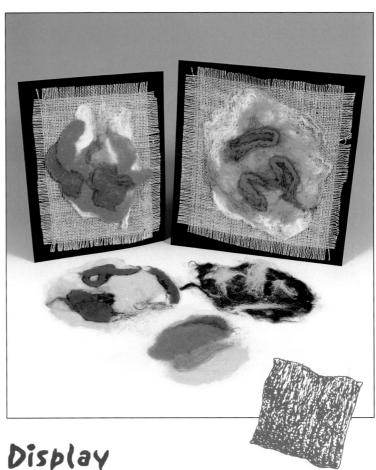

Development

● Join several small pieces of felt together to make a colourful wall hanging. Simply lay them on a sheet of bubble wrap with the edges overlapping, cover with net and rub over the joins until the fibres knit together. If necessary add a little more tops to strengthen the join.

Display

● Mount the individual pieces of felt onto contrasting coloured card or hessian and display alongside pictures of sheep.

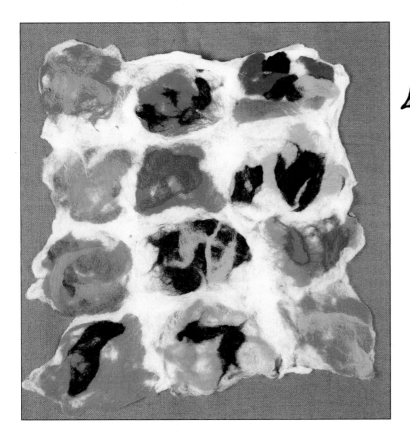

Home Links

Ask parents or carers to:

● help the children identify articles made from pure wool

● encourage the children to look for and cut out pictures of sheep in magazines and newspapers

● allow the children to collect pictures of articles that could be made from wool, such as clothing, carpets, hats, gloves and scarves.

Simply Sew

Learning Intentions

- To develop simple sewing skills.

- To develop hand/eye co-ordination.

- To introduce simple toy making techniques.

Starting Points

- Examine some simple soft toys and ask the children how they think they are made. Can they tell how many pieces have been used to make each toy?

- Examine a simple manufactured toy pattern. Establish that to make a soft toy you need at least a front and a back and some toy filler.

Designing and Making

- Cut out simple shapes from felt such as birds or animals. Alternatively, choose a seasonal theme.

- Using contrasting embroidery thread or wool encourage the children to sew randomly all over the shape adding sequins, beads or buttons to create texture.

⚠ **Note:** Supervise the use of needles.

- Dab fabric glue all around the edge of the shape on the wrong side leaving a gap where the toy is to be stuffed. Place the shape onto another piece of felt and cut it out. This is far easier than trying to match up the edges of two pre-cut shapes. When the glue is dry, stuff with a little toy filler. Glue the gap.

- If creating a toy bird, glue on brightly coloured feathers for the tail and wings.

Development

- Make simple purses and bags by cutting a rectangular shape from coloured felt. Decorate as before. Fold the bottom third up and glue into position. Fold the top third down and sew on a button to fasten. Cut a slit in the felt for the buttonhole. Make the purse into a bag by adding a handle of coloured cord.

- Stick a finished stitched shape onto coloured paper to create a card or a calendar.

Display

- Hang the birds on invisible thread in front of a window or form a mobile with wire or dowelling and create a flock of birds.

- Glue or sew loops to shapes such as snowmen, stars or trees and use as Christmas decorations.

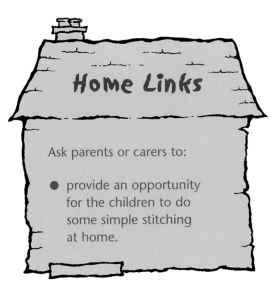

Home Links

Ask parents or carers to:

- provide an opportunity for the children to do some simple stitching at home.

Make it with Mesh

Learning Intentions

- To develop hand/eye co-ordination.

- To build on previous experience of lacing and threading.

- To experience a variety of fabrics and other materials.

- To begin to understand the difference between manufactured and natural materials.

Starting Points

- Look at examples of different kinds of net including types of rigid plastic mesh.

- Ask the children which would be the easiest net to thread something through. Do they suggest the mesh with the largest holes? Talk about what materials could be threaded through the holes.

Designing and Making

- Have ready squares of rigid plastic garden mesh (2cm square holes) and strips of brightly coloured fabric slightly wider than the piece of mesh. Make sure that the fabric passes through the holes easily but is wide enough to fill them.

- Show the children how to thread the fabric through the holes. Introduce the word 'weaving'.

- Discuss choice of colour and texture. Introduce a new strip of fabric in each row.

Development

- Instead of weaving short lines across the square, weave around all four sides, using longer strips of fabric. Work towards the centre, changing colour with each new row. Explore the diagonals.

- Introduce strips of plastic carrier bag, florist's ribbon, hair ribbon, net vegetable bags and so on.

- Make a 'Feely Curtain' by poking strips of interesting fabrics and materials through a piece of curtain or garden net. Tie on other interesting textures such as pieces of sponge (natural and synthetic), small stones and shells with holes, pieces of driftwood or interesting twigs, metal, rubber and plastic washers and small toys. Use the curtain to generate discussion about what is manufactured and what is natural.

- Tie squares of mesh together to create cubes and use these as building blocks.

Display

- Mount the woven squares onto long strips of slightly wider brightly coloured fabric or card. Use as wall hangings.

- Tie squares of mesh together to create open or lidded baskets and use for storage of small items. Glue the ends of the strips of fabric to the inside.

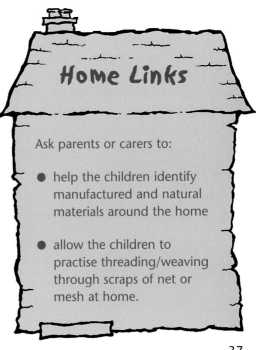

Home Links

Ask parents or carers to:

- help the children identify manufactured and natural materials around the home

- allow the children to practise threading/weaving through scraps of net or mesh at home

Creepy Creatures

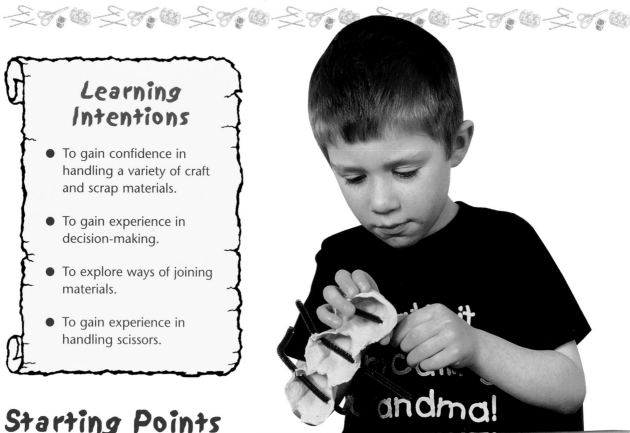

Learning Intentions

- To gain confidence in handling a variety of craft and scrap materials.

- To gain experience in decision-making.

- To explore ways of joining materials.

- To gain experience in handling scissors.

Starting Points

- Look at pictures of spiders, centipedes, woodlice and caterpillars.

- Look at the actual creatures in your school's garden.

Designing and Making

- Have available card tubes of different lengths and a variety of craft materials: cotton reels, egg boxes, yoghurt pots, pipe cleaners, string, oddments of card, wool, beads, corks, art and plastic drinking straws and bristles cut from a yard brush.

- Let the children handle the various modelling materials and consider what they could use for bodies and legs.

- Discuss ways of joining. Consider gluing, taping, stapling, poking holes and tying.

- Cut cup sections from egg boxes and use either singly or stapled together to form head and body parts.

38

- For centipedes and caterpillars staple several sections together. Poke holes in both sides of each section and push lengths of pipe cleaner through to form legs. Twist and bend.

- Wind fluffy wool around a sweet tube to create a hairy caterpillar. Glue on beads as feet. Draw a face on card and stick to the end.

Development

- Give the children an opportunity to talk to the class about their creature, to say what it eats and where it lives.

- In a large area, ask the children to discover how many ways they can move like their creature: fast or slow, close to the ground or climbing a plant.

Display

- Talk about where the creatures live and try to create a suitable habitat.

- Arrange a log and leaves on an appropriate drape. Place the creatures on and around this.

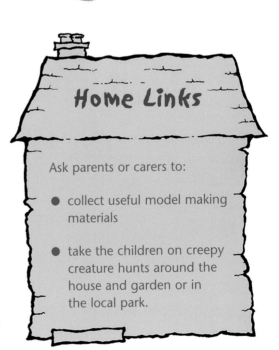

Home Links

Ask parents or carers to:

- collect useful model making materials

- take the children on creepy creature hunts around the house and garden or in the local park.

Things with Wings

Learning Intentions

- To build on previous experience of model making.

- To use scrap and craft materials creatively to make a model with wings.

- To experience different ways of joining materials.

Starting Points

- Ask the question "What things have wings?" The children will suggest everything from aeroplanes to butterflies. Explain that some birds have wings but cannot fly.

- Encourage the children to find pictures of things with wings in magazines, cut them out and make a collage.

Designing and Making

- Have available a wide range of model-making materials including card, coloured tissue, feathers, wools, fabrics, corks, coloured acetate, art straws, pipe cleaners and plasticine.

- Discuss ways of joining the various materials together.

For the wings:

- Show the children how to fold a sheet of paper and draw a pair of butterfly wings. These could be cut from coloured paper or coloured by the children.

- Bend pipe cleaners or plastic coated wire to form simple wing shapes. Glue nylon net or tissue paper to these.

- Draw wing shapes on overhead projector acetates. Make marks for veins. Cut out.

- Cut paper wing shapes and cover with coloured feathers.

For the bodies:

- Join together two egg box sections, yoghurt pots or disposable drinking cups, trapping the end of the wings in the join. Add tissue or wool tail feathers for a bird.

- Wrap a sweet tube in fur fabric to create a moth or butterfly body. Glue a pair of paper wings to the top.

Home Links

Ask parents or carers to:

- give the children opportunities to practise cutting with scissors

- encourage the children to practise drawing simple shapes on folded paper so that they create symmetrical shapes, e.g. butterfly wings.

Development

- Make kites. Tie lengths of thin string to the handles of flimsy plastic carrier bags and try flying them on a windy day.

- Make parachutes with squares of polyester cotton, thin string and large beads.

Display

- Hang some of the creatures in the role-play corner.

- Fasten lines across a corner of the classroom and dangle the creatures from these.

- Dangle the creatures from a display board in front of the children's pictures and paintings of flying things.

Fabulous Fish

Starting Points

- If possible, bring a goldfish into the class and let the children study it. Look at the fins and the tail and discuss their purpose. Ask what they think would happen if the fish jumped out of the tank. Could it move then?

- Introduce the idea of fish scales. Look at pictures of tropical fish and talk about shapes, colour and pattern.

Designing and Making

- Draw scale patterns in the bottom of two foil pie dishes using a blunt pencil. Staple the dishes together around the rim. Glue streamers of tissue, wool or raffia at one end for the tail. Stick on paper fins. Cut a 'v' shape out of the rim at the other end for its mouth.

- Use a small soft drinks bottle for a body. Tape a curtain ring to the top of the fish to suspend it. Glue on scraps of foil for scales. Add fins and a tail. Stuff clear bottles with coloured tissue or scraps of wool or fabric or squirt some squeezy paint into the bottle and roll it about to create lines and patterns.

- Join various small containers together to create longer fish bodies. Add card fins and tails.

- Make a jellyfish by stuffing a clear plastic bag with scraps of wool and screwed up clear plastic. Cut strips of bubble wrap, plastic bag and pink and purple wool and tie these into the neck of the bag.

Development

- Prepare fish shapes cut from paper-backed hessian or thick, coloured card.

- Have available trays of beads, buttons and large sequins. Ask the children to use these to glue scales all over the fish. Encourage them to make patterns with the beads.

Display

- Create an aquarium in which to display the smaller fish by cutting 'windows' in the sides of a large strong box. Paint the framework. Cut pieces of clear polythene to fit behind the 'windows'. Make plants from wool or raffene. Tape the sides of the tank in place and sprinkle gravel in the bottom of the box. Dangle the fish from thin canes.

- Create an underwater corner where the children can pretend to be divers or mermaids. Use shimmery, watery-looking drapes and dangle the 'fabulous' fish from overhead lines. Add a treasure chest of beads and bracelets.

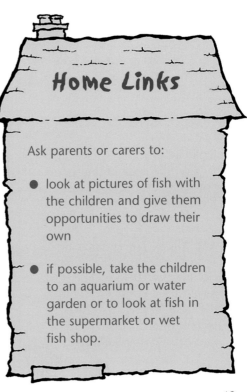

Home Links

Ask parents or carers to:

- look at pictures of fish with the children and give them opportunities to draw their own

- if possible, take the children to an aquarium or water garden or to look at fish in the supermarket or wet fish shop.

Colourful Characters

Learning Intentions

- To use a variety of craft materials to make a simple model.

- To explore ways of joining materials.

Starting Points

This theme could have numerous starting points.

- Talk about occupations. Ask the children what they would like to do when they grow up.

- Talk about nursery rhyme or favourite book characters.

- Discuss characters from favourite TV programmes.

- Discuss types of family members: mother, father, step parents, brother, sister, aunt, uncle, cousin, grand parents, great grand parents.

Designing and Making

Dish mop dolls

- Beforehand, dye the dish mops using fabric dye or coloured inks. Have ready a variety of 40cm diameter circles cut from fabric, tissue or plastic bags. Two or three circles used together make a fluffy skirt. Make a cut at the centre of the circle and push the handle of the mop through. Put glue on the handle just under the head of the mop to secure the bag. Hold in position with a little adhesive tape.

- Wind a pipe cleaner around the doll at waist level. For the arms use a long chenille pipe cleaner or art straws. Draw a face on a circle of card and glue to the flattened mop head.

Wooden spoon dolls

- Make as above but draw the face on the back of the spoon and glue on strands of wool for hair.

Tube doll with trousers

- Cut away a 10cm section from a card tube at the front and the back leaving the side pieces to form legs. The front cuts can be shaped to form feet.

44

- Glue a strip of fabric around the tube from waist level to above the shoes. Cut the strip front and back and fold the excess fabric to the inside of the tube. Glue in place. Glue another piece of fabric around half of the remaining tube to form a jacket. Cover the remaining section with paper and draw on a face. Stuff the top of the tube with tissue and glue on wool or fur fabric for hair. Use lollipop sticks, art straws or pipe cleaners for arms. Glue into position. Paint the shoes.

Tube doll with skirt

- Cut legs from a short tube and glue into an upturned bell shaped yoghurt pot. Glue another tube to the base of the pot for the body. Complete head, arms, and features as described above.

Display

- Create a street scene. Ask the children to draw buildings using wax crayon on paper. Cut these out and assemble to form a frieze. Arrange the models in groups in front of this.

- Use lumps of modelling clay to hold the mop and spoon models upright.

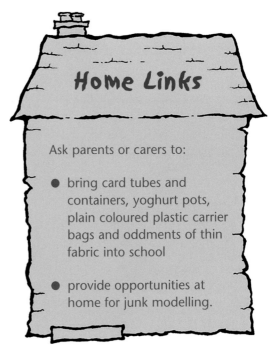

Home Links

Ask parents or carers to:

- bring card tubes and containers, yoghurt pots, plain coloured plastic carrier bags and oddments of thin fabric into school

- provide opportunities at home for junk modelling.

Jazzy Jewellery

Learning Intentions

- To experience pattern making.

- To create for a purpose.

- To explore various ways of making a piece of jewellery.

Starting Points

- All small children love dressing up. Explain that they are going to make some jewellery for the dressing up box. Ask for suggestions on how they might do this.

- Use a story about jewels or treasure as a starting point.

- Alternatively, use a special occasion as a reason for creating a gift for someone.

Designing and Making

Tin lid pendants

- Collect small tin lids. With a hammer and nail punch a hole in the lid for the thread. Spread a thick layer of PVA in the upturned lid. Fill the lid with coloured and shiny beads collected from broken necklaces.

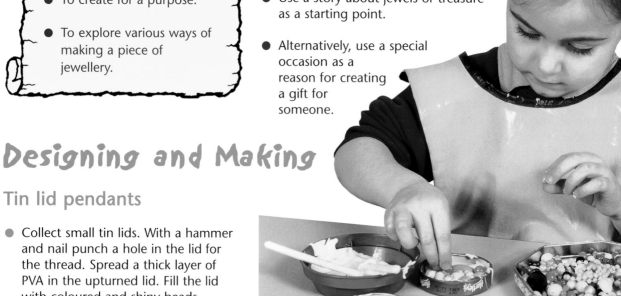

Paper pulp beads

- Shape small quantities of coloured paper pulp into bead shapes around plastic drinking straws. At the end of the session carefully remove the beads from the straws and either dry on a tray in a very low oven or dry in the microwave (see Pulp Modelling, page 20). Alternatively, leave to dry on the straws. If you are doing this, the straws need to be smeared with petroleum jelly before the beads are formed.

Pasta pendants

- Have ready pendant shapes cut from strong carton card with a hole pierced for the thread. Spread the card shape with PVA glue. Encourage the children to make a pattern on the card with different pasta shapes. Create a textured background with rice or small lentils.

- When dry, paint with metallic acrylic paints or an adult could use gold and silver spray paints.

Clay beads

- Simply roll balls of clay between the palms of the hands and pierce with a wooden skewer or similar object. For flat beads roll a sausage of clay and slice into sections. Try forming cubes of clay. Let the children experiment with forming shaped beads.

- To paint either roll in a shallow container of paint or thread onto a skewer to decorate.

Home Links

Ask parents or carers to:

- collect small tin lids

- bring into school beads from broken necklaces.

Display

- Cut head and shoulder shapes from stiff coloured paper. Ask the children to draw on the hair and features. Hang the beads around the neck and staple to the display board.

- Set lengths of plastic coated wire into a pot of plaster. Curl the ends, bend into shape and hang the pendants from this.

- Create a shop window display. Drape a piece of silk or velvet over different sized boxes. Hang some beads on mug trees. Arrange the others on the fabric.

Playful Puppets

Learning Intentions

- To develop simple toy making techniques.

- To explore a range of materials.

- To stimulate the imagination.

Starting Points

- Invite the children to bring to school any puppets they have at home. Examine and discuss the ways in which they are made.

- Have examples of stick, glove and string puppets for the children to look at.

- Ask the children if they have been to any puppet shows or seen puppets on the television.

Designing and Making

String puppets

- Puppets with skirts – cut two triangles of fabric or coloured paper. Cut four lengths of thick string or wool for the arms and legs. Glue felt hands and feet on the ends of the arms and legs. Glue the limbs to one triangle. Place a little toy filler on the centre of the triangle. Glue the other triangle on top. Glue strands of wool across the top of a cotton reel. Draw on a face with felt pen. Tie a thread to the top point of the triangle; thread this through the cotton reel and tie to a garden stick. Fasten threads to the hands and tie these to the stick.

- Puppets with trousers – cut two fabric or paper body shapes, place some toy filler between them and glue together. Thread craft pompoms or beads onto four lengths of thick string or wool to create arms and legs. Sew to the body. Glue on hands and feet. Make the head in the same way as the body. Glue in place with strong fabric glue or stitch. Attach head and arms with thread to a garden stick.

Stick puppets

- Create faces on paper plates or circles of card. Tape a garden stick or piece of dowel to the back of this. Cut a circle of fabric or plastic bag, cut a hole in the centre and push onto the stick. Glue into position under the face. Cut two finger holes in the fabric.

- Or, make a ball of paper, push a stick into this and tape in place. Cut the feet off old tights. Pull the toe of the tights over the ball. Pull one or two more layers over this. Tie or glue the tights to the stick under the ball. Glue on hair and features. Add a circle of fabric and cut finger holes as above.

Development

- Encourage the children to make up stories and have conversations with their puppets. They might like to share these with the other children.

- Make a puppet theatre from large cartons or a clothes airer and let the children take turns in 'performing'.

Display

- When not in use the stick puppets could be grouped and held upright in lumps of play dough or modelling clay.

- To display the string puppets remove the top from a large box, cut a large window in the side, create a scene inside the box and balance the puppet sticks across the top.

Home Links

Ask parents or carers to:

- help the children make simple puppets at home using a wooden spoon or an old sock.

Making Masks

Learning Intentions

- To experience a range of craft materials.

- To encourage creativity.

- To stimulate the imagination.

- To identify emotions.

Starting Points

- Show the children pictures or examples of masks from various cultures, some party masks and clown masks.

- Ask the children if the masks look sad or happy. Do the masks make the children feel other emotions? Encourage the children to express how they feel.

- Explain to the children that actors used to wear masks so that the audience could see clearly what that character was feeling.

Designing and Making

- Have ready plain paper bags large enough to fit comfortably over the children's heads. Cut the open end of the bag into a curve front and back so that it fits more comfortably over the shoulders. Cut the eyes out for them.

- Have available a wide range of craft materials to decorate the masks: wool, raffene, strips of paper, art straws, coloured feathers, circles of gummed paper, scraps of fabric, sections from egg boxes and crayons. Encourage the children to outline the eyes, add ears, a mouth, a nose, hair, maybe a bow ribbon or even a beard.

- Encourage the children to use their imaginations and to talk about their characters as they are making them.

- Create faces on large paper plates (having first cut out the eye holes). Staple or glue streamers of crêpe paper or strips of carrier bag around the top edge of the plate to cover the head and form a mane of hair. Fasten a length of elastic to the sides of the plate to hold it on the head.

Development

- Cut face shapes from coloured paper or card. Cut eyes, ears, noses and mouths from different magazine pictures and collage a face. Add wool for hair. Pierce holes in the eyes. Fasten the mask with elastic.

- Encourage the class to make up and tell stories about the different characters.

Display

- When not in use, stuff the bag masks with scrunched up newspaper and arrange on a display table.

- Pin flat masks to a wall board against brightly coloured paper. Intersperse with words about feelings: sad, happy, angry, frightened and so on.

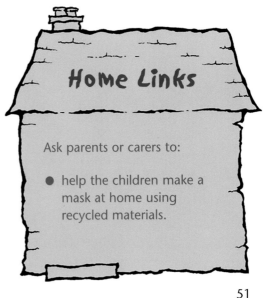

Home Links

Ask parents or carers to:

- help the children make a mask at home using recycled materials.

Fun with Flowers

Learning Intentions

- To handle a variety of craft materials.

- To learn that a flower has different parts.

- To look carefully at shapes.

Starting Points

- Bring in some flowers for the children to look at and handle. Take a flower apart to see how it is formed. Are the children familiar with the words petal, stalk and leaf?

- Compare the shapes of the flowers. Some flowers are flat and open; others are bell shaped or like pompoms. Some flowers have five petals and some have fifty!

Designing and Making

- Pierce a hole in the bottom of an egg box section and paint green. Cut circles from coloured plastic bags or tissue and glue several into the egg cup. Dip the end of a bendy drinking straw in glue and push it into the hole. Push the straw over a length of thin dowel or garden stick. Add leaves cut from plastic bags or paper.

- Cut 'v' shapes around the edges of small paper or plastic picnic bowls. Paint with acrylic or vinyl paint. Cut 'v' shapes from the rim of a bell shaped yoghurt pot and paint. Glue the pot into the bowl. Tape a garden stick to the back of the bowl. Glue paper leaf shapes around the edge of the bowl. Cover the back with a circle of green paper.

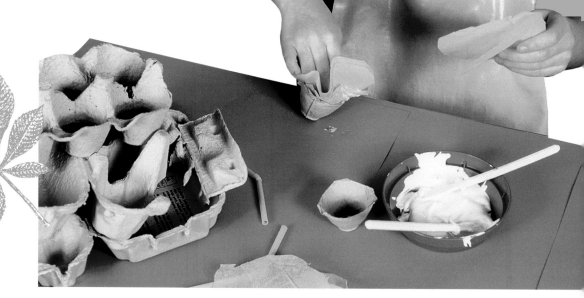

- Make climbing flowers using spent party poppers. Cut a hole in the centre of a circle of tissue or coloured plastic. Dab some glue on the shoulders of the party popper and push the circle down over the handle of the popper. Repeat this several times until a flower has formed.

- Thread a bead onto a length of wool. Using a needle, pass both ends of the thread through the hole in the handle of the party popper so that the popper rests on the bead when it is dangled on the thread.

- Tie the popper flowers at intervals to a length of coloured cord, skipping rope or washing line. Add leaves cut from felt, paper or plastic bags.

Development

- Paint pictures of flowers.

- Make collaged flowers using seeds, lentils, buttons, tissue and card.

Display

- Push some of the flowers on sticks into lumps of modelling clay to hold them upright. Cut grass shapes from green card to hide the clay.

- Set some of the sticks into plaster in coloured plant pots. Display on window sills or cupboards.

- Pin the climbing flowers around a display of paintings and collages.

Home Links

Ask parents or carers to:

- look at flowers with the children in supermarkets and florists or in parks and gardens.

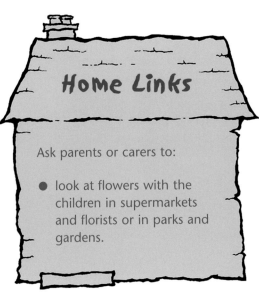

Build a Den

Learning Intentions

- To construct a free-standing structure from large cardboard tubes.

- To explore different ways of joining materials.

- To explore textures.

- To provide an opportunity for role play.

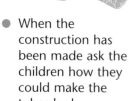

Starting Points

- What do the children understand by the word den? Have they ever built a den at home? Talk about their experiences. Lead the conversation to trees, tree houses, woods, forests and jungles. Explain that you are going to help them make a den in the classroom.

Designing and Making

- Have prepared carpet tubes cut to the desired height and lengths of wood with slits cut at suitable intervals. Slot the tops of the carpet tubes into the slits in the wood to form a structure.

- Build the structure with the children. Discuss how to arrange the tubes. Talk about enclosing a space in a square, rectangular or triangular shape.

- When the construction has been made ask the children how they could make the tubes look more like tree trunks.

- Dismantle the construction and take the tubes outside to paint or create texture by gluing on screwed up scraps of coloured paper or scraps of fabric.

● Reassemble the structure and provide strips of strong card and long narrow strips of green and brown materials such as net, chiffon, cut tights, plastic bags, fur fabric, crêpe paper and polyester cotton. Let the children glue or staple one end of each strip to the card. Staple the strips of card to the wooden supports of the den to form a walk through curtain.

● Staple a piece of camouflage or strawberry netting over the top of the structure to form a ceiling. Alternatively, show the children how to dye some net curtains.

● Make plants, flowers and creatures to decorate the den.

Development

● Encourage the children to make small-scale dens by joining smaller cardboard tubes with strips of card with slits cut into them. Create textures with fabric and tissue paper.

● Ask small groups of children to play in the den and make up a story to tell to the rest of the class.

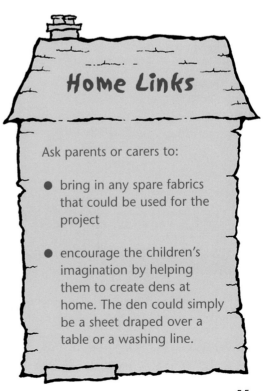

Home Links

Ask parents or carers to:

● bring in any spare fabrics that could be used for the project

● encourage the children's imagination by helping them to create dens at home. The den could simply be a sheet draped over a table or a washing line.

Playing with Polystyrene

Learning Intentions

- To introduce woodworking skills.

- To develop hand/eye co-ordination.

- To use woodworking tools safely.

Starting Points

- Show the children various woodworking tools and ask if they know the names of them and what they are used for.

- Look at some child-sized tools. Talk about how to use the tools safely.

Designing and Making

- Have available plenty of plastic tools and a few small wooden mallets. Explain the necessity of using the tools safely. Accumulate plenty of blocks of polystyrene packaging.

- Using coloured plastic golf tees as nails, encourage the children to hammer, saw, drill and so on into the polystyrene.

- Encourage the children to explain what they are doing. Ask them to identify the various tools. What are they pretending to make?

56

Development

● Introduce polystyrene ceiling tiles, plates and bowls into the woodworking area. Can the children make constructions by hammering them together with the golf tees?

● Ask the children to draw faces on upturned polystyrene bowls or plates with felt-tipped pens and hammer the coloured tees into the features. Staple strips of paper, plastic, fabric or wool around the edge for hair. Staple another plate to the back to complete the head.

● Cut a large leaf shape out of a polystyrene tile and paint it. Cut a ladybird shape out of another tile. Paint it red. When dry, glue the ladybird onto the leaf. Ask the children to use the golf tees to hammer circles of black plastic bag or fabric into the ladybird to form its spots.

⚠ **Note:** Supervise the use of woodwork tools.

Display

● Attach threads to the plate faces and dangle from the ceiling or in front of windows.

● On a display board create a paper branch against a blue sky and attach the ladybirds to this.

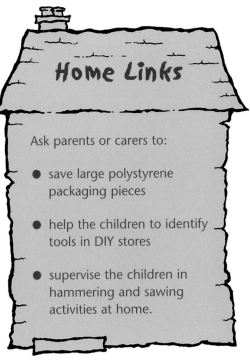

Home Links

Ask parents or carers to:

● save large polystyrene packaging pieces

● help the children to identify tools in DIY stores

● supervise the children in hammering and sawing activities at home.

Float a Boat

Learning Intentions

- To experience sawing, sanding, hammering and gluing.

- To design and make a workable model.

- To extend experience of objects that float or sink.

Starting Points

- Encourage the children to talk about boats. These might range from rowing and paddleboats in the park or fun fair to cross channel ferries, sailing and narrow boats. Have plenty of pictures of different kinds of boat to show them.

- Set out the woodwork bench. Give the children experience of sawing balsa and soft woods and hammering nails into large blocks of wood.

⚠ **Note:** Supervise the use of woodwork tools.

Designing and Making

- Have available a variety of wood off-cuts of various shapes and sizes, making sure there are no splinters but leaving some rough edges for the children to smooth down. Provide dowel of various thickness and length, glue, sandpaper and pieces of card.

- While the children are assembling their boats, encourage them to think about weight and shape. Will the boat be top heavy and topple over? Is the base wide enough, long enough or too heavy? What is the best way to join the various components – nails or glue?

Development

- Sail the boats in the water play area. Which boats float best and why? Encourage the children to give reasons.

- Design boats using materials other than wood. Use plastic bottles and containers, foil dishes and tin boxes.

- Continue the woodworking theme by building totems and wood sculptures. Provide a wooden plank and let the children glue or hammer off-cuts and wooden shapes to it. Paint in bright colours.

Display

- Float the boats in a shallow container disguised by crumpled blue tissue or fabric.

- Hammer the totems into the garden where they can be seen through the window or set in plaster in a large pot and stand in a corner of the classroom.

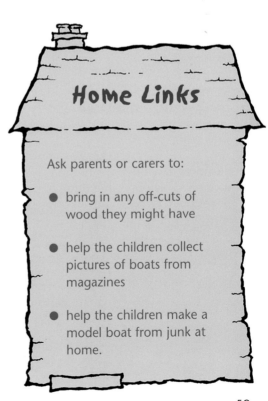

Home Links

Ask parents or carers to:

- bring in any off-cuts of wood they might have

- help the children collect pictures of boats from magazines

- help the children make a model boat from junk at home.

Building with Blocks

Learning Intentions

- To encourage large construction activities.

- To encourage language development.

- To develop spatial awareness.

- To develop imaginative play.

Starting Points

- Talk about and show pictures of how a house is built. Ask if any of the children have seen a building site. Maybe some of the children's homes have had alterations made to them and the children can talk about this. Talk about the materials used in construction and have examples to show them.

- Read stories about builders and house building. Refer to the story of 'The Three Little Pigs' and discuss which of the houses was the strongest and why.

Designing and Making

- Make textured blocks. Tape up shoeboxes of various sizes and cover with different textured materials such as textured wallpaper, hessian, sandpaper, fur fabric, carpet remnants and fake grass.

- Wrap boxes in brightly patterned wrapping paper. Extend the play by introducing a large postbox and a mailbag. Provide wrapping paper, adhesive tape and parcel bows for the children to try wrapping their own parcels.

- To make more durable blocks, stuff boxes with crumpled newspaper, tape securely with masking tape and paint with brightly coloured household vinyl paint.

- Introduce large boxes into the play area. Cut windows and doors into huge boxes. Leave some boxes open at both ends to create tunnels.

Development

● Have a 'plastic only' day when all construction is with yoghurt pots, drinking cups, margarine tubs and plastic punnets.

● Add toy hard hats, retractable tape measures, paper and pencils to the construction area to encourage role play and plan making. If possible, have some architects' plan sheets for the children to look at.

● Make 'buildings' books to keep in the construction area. Cut out pictures of different shaped buildings from magazines and paste into a scrapbook. Include pictures of detached, semi-detached and terraced houses, blocks of flats, shops, factories and farms.

Display

● Take photographs of the children's constructions and display in the construction area. Change these frequently and paste the old ones into a scrapbook or send them home with the creators.

Home Links

Ask parents or carers to:

● help the children to cover a shoebox or similar with pictures of buildings or parts of buildings such as doors and windows, for use in the construction area

● save lidded plastic containers for use in the construction area.

Machines

Learning Intentions

- To become familiar with solid shapes such as cuboid and cylinder.

- To experience a variety of ways of joining materials.

- To handle a variety of scrap materials.

- To explore how machines move.

Starting Points

- Ask the children what machines they and their families use during a day. Do they understand what a machine is?

- Talk about transport machines. How many can the children identify?

- Have a range of toys such as a digger, tractor, mower, tanker, car, vacuum cleaner and washing machine to show the children.

- Explain that they are going to make a machine using a variety of junk shapes. Explain that the machine doesn't have to work but it has to look like a machine. They can invent one if they wish or build something that they have seen before.

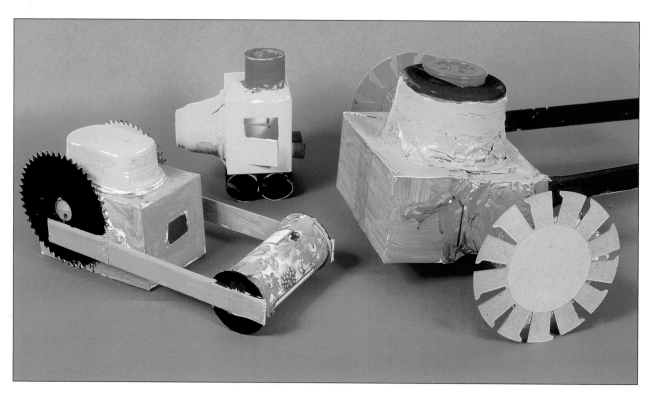

Designing and Making

- Ask the children to handle the assorted 'junk' and try out various combinations of shapes. This will help them with the designing process. It is useful to have some pre-cut card discs available for use as wheels and some strips of strong card or thin wood for use as handles.

- Discuss with the children ways of joining 3D shapes. They will probably need someone to hold the shapes together whilst they apply the tape.

- Paint the models when finished.

Development

- Experiment with moving parts, perhaps using safe real machine parts that the children can take apart and examine.

- Provide wheels and cog construction equipment for the children to create their own moving machines.

- Cut pictures of machines from catalogues and make a collage.

- Ask the children to describe the way in which the parts of a machine might move: wheels go round and round, levers go up and down, buttons go in and out. Make circles with different parts of the body, make arms and legs go up and down, and move backwards and forwards to create a machine dance.

Display

- Display garden machinery on fake grass.

- Display building and road-working machinery amongst stones, gravel and broken bricks.

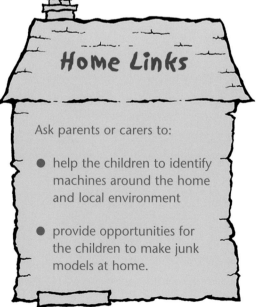

Home Links

Ask parents or carers to:

- help the children to identify machines around the home and local environment

- provide opportunities for the children to make junk models at home.

Making Masks (Page 51)